CONTENTS

FOREWORD

Not long after I started doing ventriloquism, I wrote my first comedy bit; it was a little routine with my new puppet and I performed it for my family. After I finished my father told me that my patter was terrible and that I just couldn't write comedy so I should stick to "routine books" and not try to write my own material. I was 10 years old. This proves once and for all that comedy does, indeed, come from pain.

Despite that setback, I persevered and went out and performed through my teenage years and through college. I'll never forget a time in my early 20s—I was in the middle of a show when there was a sudden, loud noise in the back of the room, surprising everyone. I tried to ad lib, but failed to get a laugh. Nothing. Nada. Crickets. I believe the Yiddish word is "bubkes." It just brought back what my father had told me—I wasn't funny on my own so I shouldn't even try.

Now the good part. In my mid-20s my luck changed dramatically when I stumbled on a little book in my local library written by Gene Perret called *Comedy Writing Step by Step* (since updated to *The New Comedy Writing Step by Step*). I checked it out and devoured it eagerly, trying to find out if I had the knack to write my own material. I read and reread it from cover to cover, taking each step very seriously, working on every exercise Gene recommended.

I clearly remember the first joke I ever wrote while working through one of Gene's comedy writing exercises. I wanted to write jokes about marriage for my puppet, Walter T. Airdale. The joke went like this:

TERRY: So Walter, I understand your anniversary was last week.

WALTER: Yep, it sure was. It was our iron anniversary.

TERRY: Which anniversary is that?

WALTER: I forgot our anniversary and she hit me with an iron!

Not a great joke, but it was life-changing for me. With that one joke I realized that I had the ability to write my own material! I kept at it; I would use Gene's book as my comedy bible and do the exercises constantly. As a result, two things happened. The jokes started to flow faster and faster, while the enormous emotional brakes my father had put me under began to disappear. I could write a funny joke!

A few years and much hard work later that joke-writing confidence and ability enabled me to ad-lib as well, always getting a laugh when the unexpected happened during my show. And it all came from my hard work and dedication to the principles Gene had laid down in his books.

Gene's new book, *The Ten Commandments of Comedy*, ties together all the lessons I learned from his past books and workshops. It's an amazing tool that contains the main rules of comedy for anyone who wants to make a career as a comedy writer, performer, public speaker, or even for someone who just wants to be funnier in living rooms. Regardless of which describes who you are, you should read and review this book regularly.

I am living proof that these rules and principles work, because decades after that fateful day when I discovered and read that book by Gene Perret, I won *America's Got Talent* and now am the headliner in my own theater at the Mirage in Las Vegas.

Thanks, Gene! I hope this in some small way lets you know how much your teachings changed my life. And for all of you who are starting to fulfill you own dream by reading *The Ten Commandments of Comedy*—good luck! You are Luke Skywalker about to be taught by the Jedi master Yoda of comedy writing: Gene Perret.

—Terry Fator

INTRODUCTION

Anything that works does so because it follows those principles that make it work. An airplane flies because it is built according to the principles that govern flight. A clock keeps accurate time because it's manufactured to follow the rules that govern timekeeping. The lights go on when you hit the wall switch in your home because they're wired in accordance with laws governing electricity. If these items didn't follow the rules, they wouldn't work.

There are fundamentals, too, that apply to comedy—rules that must be followed. Some may object that comedy should be free-flowing, improvisational, creative. "I don't want to follow rules," they might say. "I just want to do what I want to do to make people laugh. Following some set of *regulations* would inhibit my originality." It's a faulty argument. Would you want to fly to Pittsburgh in a plane that was built by someone who said, "I don't want to follow rules. I just want to build airplanes the way I want to build them?" Probably not. It's almost certain that you'd rather fly in one that gets off the ground and stays off it for as long as the pilot wants.

Does adhering to established principles inhibit originality? There are countless types and models of airplanes: single-engine aircraft, giant passenger planes, stealth bombers, huge cargo transports, and hundreds of other variations. Despite their differences, they all fly because they follow the principles of flight. There's no foreseeable limit to the inventiveness of aeronautical engineers and the machines they will create, yet you can be certain the remarkable aircraft of the future will still follow the principles of flight.

Again, though, some may argue that these examples— airplanes, clocks, and lights—are mechanical. Mechanical items are obliged to follow physical principles. Creative artists, though, should be free of such restrictions. For artists to follow rules, these people might claim, would be to limit their creativity, their genius.

Music, though, is a creative art. There are brilliant classical composers, great song writers, and innovative musicians who work in jazz, rhythm and blues, heavy metal, and so on. Yet all of them are governed by strict, mathematical principles. Scales are well defined. Chords that harmonize with the melody are controlled. Play according to those rules and you can create beautiful music in whichever genre you prefer. Break those rules and the music sounds discordant.

Knowing the principles of music frees rather than inhibits the musician. Many people can pick up a guitar and readily play hundreds of songs by learning just three, maybe four, basic chords. By studying the principles that govern music, though, a musician can then add depth, variation, and charm to the music. If Beethoven had been limited to using three or four basic chords, he might have played some cute ditties for his friends to sing along with at dinner parties, but he could never have written his symphonies and would never have become a musical legend.

The more you know about your craft, the better you can master it . . . and the more enjoyment you can bring to yourself and to others.

A key benefit of knowing the principles of your craft is that it allows you to search back and find flaws in your work. It also gives you the knowledge you need to then correct those problems. It's always interesting in sports that regardless how well athletes perform, they always insist that they can improve something or other in their performance. How do they do that? Invariably, they return to basics. Knowing what principles apply to their sport, they can check to make sure they're following those rules and apply corrective measures when needed.

A well received comedy performance is a tremendous high. However, a weak performance is depressing. Comedians say "I bombed" or "I died"—it feels that traumatic. Knowing the rules of comedy allows the humorist to analyze the material or the presentation and discover why the performance bombed, and what must be done to repair it. It's an effective way to convert a poor or mediocre comedy bit into a one that will have the audience in stitches.

There are rules, precepts, principles, regulations, standards, fundamentals—whatever you want to call them—that control the effectiveness of comedy. I've chosen to call them "commandments." Admittedly, it's in part a gimmick to get your attention. But *The Ten Commandments of Comedy* has a biblical tone to it, a sort of threat from above that might be ignored only at one's peril.

The precepts that follow in this book are the rules that govern making people laugh. There are ten of them, but the order in which they're listed is irrelevant. For your humor to be effective, you should adhere to all of them. If, for some reason, a joke or a routine doesn't seem to be producing the results you think it should, it would be wise to review each of the commandments to try to find out where you're violating or bending the rules.

No one can really explain why people laugh or what prompts them to laugh. People in the profession have timidly accepted that.

"The jokes didn't work tonight."

"Why not?"

"I don't know. The people just didn't laugh."

Suppose you took a watch to the repair shop and asked the jeweler to have a look at it. You say, "Do you know what's wrong with this watch?"

"Yeah, it's not working."

"Why is it not working?"

"I don't know. It's just not working."

You ask, "Does it need a new battery? Does it need cleaning? Does it need winding? Are the gears jammed? What?"

"It's just not working."

We wouldn't accept that from a watch repair shop, but too often we accept it about our comedy routines. It's simply a mystery that we learn to live with. But that mystery generates a fear. It's like trying to navigate in a completely darkened room. Many people hesitate to use humor because of this fear. Speakers sometimes say that they're afraid to open with a joke because no one ever laughs at their jokes.

Learning and being aware of the Ten Commandments of Comedy can brighten that metaphorical darkened room. Comedians and comedy writers can learn *why* their material needs improvement and where the changes should be made. The Ten Commandments are a checklist you can use to review your presentation. With them, you can now find out why the watch isn't working and do something to correct the defect.

There's a story about a gentleman who was a fabulous basketball free-throw shooter. He would often give demonstrations where, blindfolded, he would make shot after shot. One time, he demonstrated his skills and Bill Sharman, the Hall-of-Fame guard who played for the Boston Celtics, was present. Sharman was the league leader in free throws for many years while he played. After the demonstration, this man asked Bill Sharman how he could improve his free-throw shooting talents. Bill Sharman said, "Take off the blindfold."

That's what these Ten Commandments will do for you. They'll help you improve your comedy ability by taking off the blindfold.

I

Thou Shalt Surprise

Surprise is such an essential element of comedy that if your joke, story, anecdote, or piece of business doesn't have a twist or a surprise to it, it's not comedy. Perhaps the only exception to this is if you get a laugh and then elongate it, keep repeating it, or refer back to it occasionally. Even then, though, the laughter is built on the surprise of the initial gag.

The craft of stage magic is a good illustration of the use of surprise and it parallels the way comics use the same principle. When the magician is locked in chains inside a bag and sealed within a locked trunk, his beautiful assistant stands on the trunk, lifts a curtain around herself and suddenly, almost instantaneously, drops the curtain. In that fraction of a second, she is gone and the magician stands on the trunk. When that moment happens there is an audible gasp from the audience. Wow! That is unbelievable. Surprise is part of every magic illusion, and it should be part of every bit of comedy that's done—and the impact should be just as astounding as the audience's amazement at the magician's skill.

Magicians rarely reveal the secret behind their tricks. Why? Because if the audience knows how the illusion is executed, there is no longer any surprise. Consequently, there's little entertainment value.

What is surprise? It's the unexpected, the twist, the sudden change of direction. W.C. Fields said once that comedy is when you expect something to break and it only bends. Some people contend that comedy is a battle of wits with your audience. Each of you is trying to outwit the other. Generally, the comic wins and the audience laughs in acknowledgment of how they've been duped. There's truth to that because most people in an audience try to write the finish of the joke before the comic can utter it. However, the comedian, with good material, preparation, and knowing where he or she is headed, should out-clever the audience.

Timing is an important facet of surprise. You want to give the listeners time to start thinking of a punch line, but not enough time to outdo you, the comedian. This is like trying to upset someone by pulling the rug out from under them. That's certainly a surprise, but only if you time it right. Of course, if you tell the victims that you're going to surprise them, you won't be able to pull off the gag because they won't step onto the rug. However, even if you do dupe them onto the rug, you still have to time your action properly. Pull it too soon, and they won't be standing on it yet. Pull it too late, and they'll be gone when you pull it. Pull it at the exact right time—surprise!

There are several techniques for generating the surprise.

One device comics use is to misdirect the audience—to lead them like the Pied Piper, then suddenly change direction on them. Henny Youngman's classic, among the most perfect one-liners ever written, employed misdirection:

Take my wife ... please.

The first three words lead everyone to believe the comic is saying, "Let's use my wife as an example." But no. With that fourth word, he lets his listeners know that he is literally pleading for someone to take his wife. The misdirection is wonderfully effective.

Consider also this line from Rita Rudner:

> *I love being married. It's so nice to find that one person you want to annoy for the rest of your life.*

It certainly starts out on a positive note, but Rita was only playing with our minds, misdirecting our thoughts.

Shock is another technique for creating surprise. Blue humor falls into this category. When stuck for an ad lib or a punch line, some comics use shocking language. It gets laughs because listeners are surprised that anyone would use that language in public. Insults are another form of shock laughter. Don Rickles may say to another performer:

> *I've known you for a long time, right? We go back a long ways. I must tell you in all sincerity, I never liked you.*

We laugh at that because it's shocking, surprising, that one person would so blatantly say that to another.

One actor who did a Mark Twain performance would enter from the back of the hall, unannounced and unnoticed by the audience. From there he would pronounce loudly:

> *This is the worst looking crowd I've ever seen.*

People laugh and applaud at the unusual beginning of the performance. During the applause, "Twain" ambles to the front of the hall and onto the stage. When the applause dies down, he gazes out at the audience and says:

> *You don't look a heluva lot better from up here.*

It's so audacious and shocking that it generates a very appreciative laugh from the onlookers.

Traditional comedy wisdom advises putting the key word at the end of the sentence because this technique enhances the element of surprise. It's similar to cracking a whip: You can swing a whip as hard as you want, but it will not crack until you change its direction. It's the sudden snapping of the whip in the opposite direction that causes the loud report. Similarly, your comedy will crackle when you have that surprise close to the end of the sentence. There is a book titled *Marriage is Forever... Some Days Longer*. It's the last word that gets that whip to crack.

It's not always possible to put the punch word at the very end of the sentence, but as the following joke demonstrates, it still helps to get it as near to the end as possible:

> *My friend is so cheap, he not only has the first dollar he ever made, but also the arm of the man who handed it to him.*

Sometimes simply revealing keen or eccentric observations to an audience furnishes the surprise. The humorist mentions some phenomenon that should have been obvious, but no one except the humorist seems to have noticed it. The surprise is when the audience realizes that they should have seen this before. It's true. It was right before their eyes, but they failed to recognize it so they laugh in surprise when the comic points it out. Jerry Seinfeld's observation falls into this category:

> *You know what I don't understand. Why do skydivers wear helmets?*

George Carlin also asks:

> *Why do we park on driveways and drive on parkways?*

Another simple way of furnishing surprise is by a sudden change of expression, pitch, or loudness. Sometimes a comedian can just make a face and it gets a laugh. It's an expression we didn't expect. Often a comic will speak in a normal voice and then shout for some reason or another. The change of volume is a surprise. As a standup comic, Jim Carrey peppered his routines with goofy, ridiculous faces and poses. They got laughs. Picture the antics of Harpo Marx. He never spoke professionally, but some of his sudden and surprising moves and faces were hilarious.

Another technique is to surprise the audience by allowing them to mentally complete your joke for you. Imply your punch line rather than coming right out and declaring it. Say it by not saying it. The surprise here comes from the audience automatically supplying your intended punch line and taking great pleasure in doing so. The following Henny Youngman gag is a good example of this technique:

> *I haven't spoken to my wife in three years. I didn't want to interrupt.*

Notice that the comic doesn't come out and say that his wife talks a lot. However, his meaning is abundantly clear. The audience "gets it." They're proud of having "gotten it," and they laugh.

Here's a brilliant Rita Rudner line that also illustrates this technique very well:

> *I was going to have cosmetic surgery until I noticed that the doctor's office was full of portraits by Picasso.*

Rudner doesn't say why she changed her mind about having the cosmetic surgery performed, but the audience figures it out. Having figured it out provides a nice, pleasant surprise that generates laughter.

There are many other ways to amaze, astound, and surprise an audience. Each comic may develop his or her own arsenal of tricks. More than the specific techniques, though, the key element here is to remember that if you want people to laugh at whatever you're saying or doing, there'd better be a surprise in there for them. It's the First Commandment of Comedy.

II

THOU SHALT BE TRUTHFUL

Humor must be based on truth. Regardless of how wacky, bizarre, outlandish, or downright crazy your punch line is, it must spring from a truthful premise. Consider the following routine:

> As I was driving the other day, I noticed that nowadays in ninety percent of the cars people are taking a nap while they're driving. I don't know what's causing this. They must be mixing Sominex in with our gasoline, or something.
>
> I'm sure you've noticed it, too. Drivers are sleeping all over the place. The highway looked like a pajama party at 65 miles an hour.
>
> I thought the guy behind me was honking his horn. Turns out he was just snoring loudly.
>
> I didn't know what to do, so I turned off the car radio. I didn't want to wake anybody.

This is a routine based on a false premise. People are *not* falling asleep while they're driving in epidemic proportions. Listeners know it's not true…and, in fact, know it couldn't be true. No matter how good the jokes are, they're not good enough if they're not based on truth, or even a perceived truth.

An audience would react to this routine by questioning it. Listeners would be saying to themselves, "I've never noticed when I was driving that most of the other drivers were asleep." They'd spend more of their time trying to relate this routine to reality than they would to appreciating the lines that were based on it.

The premise simply isn't true and the audience recognizes that. All of the lines that are based on this false proposition are therefore tainted. Regardless of the cleverness and the structure of the gags, they fail because the audience rebels against the foundation that supports them.

Truth, in this sense, doesn't mean the "raise your right arm and swear on the Bible" sort of truth that you would pledge in a courtroom. No humorist will ever be tried for perjury because some of his or her one-liners were not factually correct. The truth as it applies to joke telling can be exaggerated, distorted, or carried to an extreme limit. Nevertheless, there should be a recognizable element of truth present for the audience to appreciate the comedy—to have some frame of reference to base the humor on. For instance, look at the following routine:

> *Have you heard about all the shootings on the Los Angeles Freeways? It's a new fad that L.A. has introduced to the country—Snipers on Wheels.*

> *New cars in L.A. now come equipped with air bags and flak jackets.*

> *They have different signals in Los Angeles. When a guy puts his hand out the window, if it*

doesn't have a gun in it, it means he's going to turn left.

I have a bumper sticker on my car that says, "Honk if you're unarmed."

Los Angeles is a western city where seldom is heard a discouraging word because if you say one, the guy in the next car may shoot at you.

It's certainly not true that all the drivers in Los Angeles are packing handguns. It's not a fact that they're issuing cars equipped with flak jackets. But, at the time when these gags were used, it was true that there had been some gun incidents on the Los Angeles freeways which had been widely reported in the papers. Consequently, these exaggerations and distortions were based on a recognizable fact.

Often the truth can be so ironic that merely stating it provides the comedy. For instance, George Carlin questioned:

Why do they put expiration dates on sour cream?

Jerry Seinfeld observed:

Nothing in life is "fun for the entire family."

Oscar Wilde said:

Always forgive your enemies. Nothing annoys them so much.

All of these lines state a truth. The listeners recognize the reality and appreciate the irony.

Sometimes the truth provides the comedy, but the humorist has to arrange the words into a joke form. For example:

> *Insanity is hereditary. You catch it from your kids.*

> *Can you imagine what car insurance rates would be for test dummies?*

> *A smart husband buys his wife fine china so she won't trust him to wash it.*

Or another of Oscar Wilde's famous lines:

> *Bigamy is having one wife too many. So is marriage.*

Fundamentally, it's the truth in the above statements that furnishes the humor. To show why the truth is so important to these lines, let's change the last one, Oscar Wilde's comment, just a bit:

> *Bigamy is having one wife too many. So is bachelorhood.*

There's no longer any truth to that statement. Now, it's not funny. In the original example, the humorist is saying that bigamy is having too many spouses. The punch line is saying that having even one wife is too many. That's the irony in the comment. However, it's not true that the irony applies also to a bachelor because a bachelor has no wives.

Below is a wonderful routine (paraphrased) that comic Stanley Myron Handelman once presented. It's interesting to note how most of the setup material is obviously untrue, yet the routine is saved by relating it to a concept that we can all accept as founded in truth.

> *I had a dog once. It was my favorite pet. But then one day it got hit by a car. I took it to a number of vets, but they all said they couldn't save my little pet. But then I found one veterinarian who said he could try an operation. It was an experiment, but it might save my dog's life. So he did the operation. He made like a little cut in the dog's throat and did something, but whatever he did saved the animal's life. The dog lived and was fine. But the strange thing was that after the operation, my dog could talk—just like a human being. But then I had to get rid of him. All he ever talked about was his operation.*

We don't believe much of this tale at all. We hardly accept that the dog could speak just like a human being. Yet, the element of truth at the end turns it into a beautiful comedy routine. We all accept the truth—even if it is an exaggerated truth—that people love to talk about their operations *ad nauseum*.

This Second Commandment dictates that comedy—even if it's bizarre, strange, incredible, wacky, goofy, exaggerated, distorted, and carried to an extreme—must at some point or another be based on truth.

III

Thou Shalt Be Understood

Listed below are two good gags. Read them over and compare:

> *J'ai un grand régime. Vous pouvez manger tout ce que vous voulez, mais vous devez le manger avec les gens nus gras.*

> *Glauben Sie im Aberglaube nicht—er bringt das Unglück.*

Which of the two do you prefer? Which do you think is the funniest? Which do you think would be best received by an audience? Unless you're fluent in French or understand German, you probably can't decide.

In truth, neither one is probably very funny to you. Why? Because you can't understand them. You have no idea what either one is saying.

They're both fine gags, but not to someone who can't read them.

Admittedly, it's a bit unfair to ask you to evaluate gags that are written in languages that are foreign to you. And it's surely not often that you'll be writing gags in a strange language or standing in front of a crowd who can't understand what you're saying because they don't comprehend your native tongue. Nevertheless, these sample gags make the point that if your comedy line is not understood by the listeners, it's not a comedy line.

Here are a few more well-constructed, inventive, audience-tested lines that were effective. And they are in the English language. Read and evaluate these:

> *People here have asked me not to mention the 39-16s. They didn't have to bother. The only thing I know about a 39-16 is that it's half of a really built girl.*

> *Charlie is a very handy man with a hammer and a saw. You didn't think Bob got those haircuts at a barbershop, did you?*

> *Herb Frickman is a very unusual guy to talk to on the phone. He's the only guy in the building that you can hang up on without losing volume.*

These gags, too, probably read like a foreign language to you. They worked well when they were used in context, but to you, at this moment, they're worthless comedically. You have no idea what or about whom the comic is speaking. Consequently, the gags don't produce laughs.

To justify these lines, let me explain them:

The first was delivered at a workplace that was having work related problems. There was a contract dispute between a small group of workers and the hierarchy of the company. It was a fierce battle and much of it was waged in the company newspaper and bulletins that this group of workers published. In the contract, these dissatisfied workers were referred to as 39-16s. Because of the many reports, everyone in the company was familiar with the litigation and the term "39-16." This audience, aware of the context, recognized and appreciated what the emcee that day was saying. However, to anyone unfamiliar with the background, the joke is meaningless.

The second gag was at a testimonial dinner for a gentleman named Charlie. Charlie worked with a partner named Bob, and everyone at the dinner knew that these two were inseparable in the workplace. They also knew that Charlie liked to work on home repair projects, and they knew, too, that Bob had an old-fashioned crew cut. They completely got the meaning when the emcee implied that Charlie, with his hammer and saw, gave Bob those haircuts. The humor was recognized by this particular audience; it confuses any audience who doesn't know these people or the back story.

The third line was also delivered at a dinner, this one honoring Herb Frickman. Herb was known to have an extremely loud voice when conversing on the phone. All of his friends in the audience knew that and laughed at the comic's one-liner. People who didn't know Herb wouldn't understand the joke at all.

Audiences cannot laugh at a joke if they don't know it's a joke. They can't laugh at a concept that they don't comprehend. Therefore, every part of your humor—the premise, the references, and the wording—must all be understood before the gag can be effective.

One comedian was scheduled to give a performance in a foreign country. In doing the research, the writers learned that this nation did not have a problem with homeless people. The situation simply didn't exist in their nation. So the comic and his staff prepared several gags about what a blessing it was not to have the blight of homelessness, but none of the material worked because the listeners were not familiar with homelessness. They had no idea what it was. Consequently, gags based on that topic were not *understood* by the listeners. The premise must be understood for the comedy to be effective.

References that are used in connection with a comedy line must also be understood by the audience. For instance, in commenting on those people who have to testify and respond to penetrating questions at a congressional hearing, you might say:

> *It must be tough being a witness at those Congressional hearings. The next day you must feel like you've been in a 12-round match with Mike Tyson.*

Okay. Most listeners would comprehend that statement because they know who Mike Tyson is. As a witness, you'd feel beat up. In fact, beat up by one of the heaviest punchers in boxing.

However, compare that to the following line:

> *It must be tough being a witness at those Congressional hearings. You probably wind up feeling like a chunk of calcium oxalate undergoing lithotripsy.*

The comparison is valid and the image is appropriate. However, very few in the audience would appreciate that because the references are too obscure. Only a small percentage would realize that the comic is talking about a kidney stone that's being blasted apart by a treatment that utilizes shock waves to break it into small chunks.

The references must be obvious and understandable to get laughter from an audience.

Earlier we listed some gags that were written in foreign languages. Obviously, they'd be useless for a mass

American audience. However, not all English language words are understood by an English speaking audience. The words used should not obscure the comic's meaning or even confuse it. Take, for example, this Steven Wright line:

> I went down the street to the 24-hour grocery.
> When I got there, the guy was locking the front door.
> I said, "Hey, the sign says you're open 24 hours."
> He said, "Yes, but not in a row."

That's a funny line and the meaning is obvious to the listeners. Consider the following variation, though:

> I went down the street to the 24-hour grocery.
> When I got there, the guy was locking the front door.
> I said, "Hey, the sign says you're open 24 hours."
> He said, "Yes, but not in a chronologically consecutive sequence."

It might be understood by some; not understood by others. In any case, though, it confuses the gag. For comedy to be effective, the audience should understand the words in the gag—especially in the punch line.

Another important aspect of being understood applies to those who deliver comedy—emcees at banquets or stand-up comedians, for example. The audience must clearly hear and understand what you are saying. A punch line that is garbled has no power. This George Carlin line is an example of that, as translated to the written page:

> *I just had a chest X-ray and they found a spot*
> *on my lungs. Fortunately it turned out to be*
> *bnarbguesosh.*

That line means nothing. It can't be understood. Yes, it's written on paper, but it's equivalent to a spoken joke where the key word is unintelligible. Isn't it a much funnier gag this way:

> *I just had a chest X-ray and they found a spot*
> *on my lungs. Fortunately it turned out to be*
> *barbecue sauce.*

Now it makes sense. You can read it. As a spoken joke, you can decipher the punch line.

As a vocal humorist, you must be certain to deliver your punch lines in a clear and distinct voice. It's your responsibility to speak intelligibly and enunciate properly. Be aware, too, of the speed of your speech. Sometimes comics rehearse so much and are so proud of their clever quips that they rush to get them out to the eager audience. As a result, many of the key words are jumbled. Again, using Carlin's line as an example, it might look like this:

> *I just had a chest X-ray and they found*
> *a spot on my lungs. Fortunatelyitturned*
> *outtobebarbecuesauce.*

The words are there, but it's difficult for the audience to appreciate them enough to generate spontaneous laughter. Certainly, comics will develop a particular delivery style that may violate some precepts of proper grammar and oratory. That's a prerogative of the comic. However, if that delivery produces punch lines that are impossible to hear or decipher, it hurts the comedy.

Oh, yes … here are translations for the two jokes at the beginning of this chapter:

(The one in French) I have a great diet. You can eat all you want, but you have to eat it with naked fat people.

(And the one in German) Don't believe in superstition—it brings bad luck.

See. Aren't they more entertaining when you can understand them? That's why the Third Commandment of Comedy says, "Thou shalt be understood."

IV

Thou Shalt Be Current

In 1960, the film *Sons and Lovers* was nominated for an Academy Award as Best Picture of the Year. Bob Hope emceed the Oscar telecast that year and said of this picture:

> *One of the Best Picture Nominees this year is* Sons and Lovers. *I think it's the story of Bing Crosby's family.*

That was a powerful line in Hope's monologue because the movie was well-known, Hope and Crosby were notorious for taunting one another, and Crosby's four boys had gained a reputation for mischief. However, it was a powerful line back then. Today, it means practically nothing. Hardly anyone remembers that there even was a film called *Sons and Lovers*. Bob Hope, Bing Crosby, and Crosby's four sons from his first marriage are all gone. The joke is gone.

On September 25, 1962, Sonny Liston gained the heavyweight championship of the world by knocking out Floyd Patterson two minutes and six seconds into the first round. A few days later, comedian Slappy White added these gags to his routine:

*I had a party the other night. I was going to
invite Floyd Patterson and Sonny Liston, but the
last time they got together they almost had a fight.*

*I had a $100 seat for that fight and Patterson,
he sat down before I did.*

*That fight was so short, when they raised Liston's
arm, I thought it was a deodorant commercial.*

*But I'd like to see both of those fighters come
back ... and finish that first round.*

That routine was funny for the week or two after the
well-publicized, much written-about fight. It was current
then. It was what people were talking about. A few weeks
later, it wasn't as funny. Today, it's simply nostalgia, if
that.

For topical material to be effective, it must be current.
This is not to imply that all comedy must be topical and
current. There are two types of comedy lines, the first
being those that are topical, based on events that are
happening now. These can be events from the entertainment or sports worlds, from politics, from science, from
the gossip columns, and so on. In short, they can be
anything that you might read about in today's newspa-
pers or anything that people are discussing.

The lines listed above are examples of that type of
humor.

But there is also generic comedy. Here the premises are
virtually timeless. Consider these lines:

Ask your child what he wants for dinner only if he's buying.
　　—Fran Lebowitz

I want my children to have all the things I never had ... and then move in with them.
　　—Phyllis Diller

I can't cook. I use a smoke alarm as a timer.
　　—Carol Siskind

My wife wanted a fur coat, but I wanted a new car. So we compromised. We bought a fur coat, but we keep it in the garage.
　　—Henny Youngman

These are lines that have a long shelf life. They're funny now; they'll be funny a long time from now. They're not limited by the freshness of the headlines because they're not based on headlines or talk around the water cooler or what is happening right now. These are premises that are practically eternal.

If you work in this area of comedy, your work is ageless. It always seems up-to-date. However, if you do include premises or references that are dependent on present day events, then those events must be current. If they're not, your material feels tired and worn. Your creativity is suspect because you're reaching back and trying to resurrect topics that are now not as interesting as they once were. . .or that have been forgotten entirely.

It's almost like having a pleasant looking garden. There are two types of flowers you can grow: perennials or annuals. Perennials are forever. With the help of nature's sunshine and rain, they will flourish and bloom around the same time each year. Your garden always looks fresh and beautiful.

Annuals though are not that cooperative. You plant them and they bloom and look gorgeous for one season. After that, they die. If you don't replant periodically, then you'll have a garden that looks dead. To keep a garden that looks fresh and beautiful, you must constantly replace the old with the new.

That's what you must do with topical material. Revitalize it, replenish it, add contemporary references. One comedian came up with some lines that explained how awkward he felt in a certain situation where he was surrounded by "better" people. These lines worked well for him:

I feel like Chester in a roomful of Matt Dillons.

I feel like Twiggy in a roomful of Dolly Partons.

Today, those lines need an explanation. At the time these lines were used, there was a popular TV show on the air called *Gunsmoke*. In it, Matt Dillon (played by James Arness) was the Marshall, who was strong, brave, and self-assured. Chester (played by Dennis Weaver) was his deputy, who walked with a limp, carried no gun, and was not nearly as powerful a presence as Dillon.

Twiggy was a very much promoted fashion model who was quite thin and flat-chested. Dolly Parton was a country singer who was known as much for her large bosom as she was for her talented singing.

Both of the above lines worked well—back then. The form of the lines would still be effective today, but the comic would have to find contemporary names that would replace Chester and Matt Dillon, and Twiggy and Dolly Parton. Or you could do what the late comic

George Gobel did. He expressed the same idea using timeless references. His line would work as well today as it did in the '70s when he first used it on *The Tonight Show*. Gobel sat on the couch with legendary entertainers Bob Hope, Dean Martin, and Johnny Carson. He said:

> *Do you ever get the feeling that the whole world is a tuxedo and you're a pair of brown shoes?*

Some lines that are contemporary can have a second, third, or fourth life because history repeats itself. For instance, consider the lines before about the Sonny Liston-Floyd Patterson boxing match. Suppose there's another highly promoted fight in which boxer A knocks out boxer B early in the first round (some of Mike Tyson's fights in the '80s, for example). Then all of the lines listed above apply, except that you substitute "Boxer A" for "Sonny Liston" and you substitute "Boxer B" for "Floyd Patterson." You now have a fresh, current, funny routine about the fight that just happened.

It's also worth noting that there are certain items that have transcended the comedy "statute of limitations." These are particular events that happened long ago, yet are not considered dated. For example, Custer's Last Stand, the sinking of the *Titanic*, and so on. Referring to events like these in your comedy—if, of course, it's done in a funny and clever way—doesn't label your humor as out of date.

So the Fourth Commandment of Comedy—"Thou Shalt Be Current"—does not dictate that every comedy line must be current or topical. It does insist, though, that any premises or any references that you utilize be reasonably up-to-date. If they're not, your act may be labeled as tired, worn, or hackneyed. If the gags and references are "today," your act will be considered sharp, up-to-date, and cutting-edge. Every humorists craves those adjectives.

V

THOU SHALT BE CONCISE

William Shakespeare says in Act II, Scene 2 of
Hamlet that "Brevity is the soul of wit." Despite the
Bard's admonition, shorter gags are not, by definition,
more powerful than longer ones. Consider once again
Henny Youngman's classic, short, funny line:

>   *Take my wife … please.*

That's a solid joke that is only four words long. Would
it be funnier if Youngman had said:

>   *My wife … please.*

Better yet, how about if he simply said:

>   *Wife … please.*

Of course, he might have shortened the line to its bare
essential and said only:

>   *… please.*

Obviously, none of these shortened variations pack
the comedy punch of the original four-word gag. Surely
one word is shorter than four words. But one word is not
necessarily more comedically effective than four words.

This Fifth Commandment—"Thou Shalt Be
Concise"—does not necessarily mean "Thou Shalt Be

Shorter." Well, then, what does it mean? It means that a joke is most effective when it is as short as it can be and still remain a joke.

Review the Henny Youngman example. It's four words long and it is a joke. Remove any one, two, or three words from it and it admittedly becomes shorter, but it's no longer a funny line. It's no longer a joke.

Any piece of comedy requires a certain amount of information to set up the punch line. There must be some frame of reference that the comic uses the punch line to play against. For example, George Carlin once joked:

> *Why do they lock gas station bathrooms? Are they afraid someone will clean them?*

In order for the audience to appreciate the cleverness of that punch line, they must know that the comic is referring to gas station restrooms. That information is essential to *get* the joke. The punch line only makes sense if it refers back to "gas station bathrooms." In order for the listeners to make that connection, they must know about it. How do they know about it? The comic must tell them.

So with any gag, the comic must give the listeners enough information to understand the irony of the punch line. The two elements are essential. You can't have a punch line without a setup; you can't have a setup if there is no punch following it.

For example, take Steven Wright's line:

> *I had a friend who was a clown. When he died, all his friends went to the funeral in one car.*

The setup line alone is not funny. No audience would laugh at that. And the punch line alone is not funny. In fact, it's confusing. The audience would not only not laugh, but they would be bewildered. They'd wonder why people would go to a funeral in only one car. They'd wonder what the comic was talking about. They'd wonder about his or her sanity.

Together, though, the setup and the punch line form a wonderfully amusing gag.

One comedian tells the story of landing a coveted guest shot on a high-rated variety show. It was the kind of guest spot that could launch a mid-level comedian into stardom. It was a remarkable opportunity, so the comic worked hard on the right material for that gig. However, on the night of the telecast, the show was running long. The powerful host of the show decided to make some quick cuts. He decided on his own to shorten the comic's act by eliminating the parts that he felt were not funny.

In effect, what he did was cut out all the setup lines. In his mind, he was leaving the funny parts in—the punch lines. He didn't realize that by taking out the essential straight lines, he was rendering the punch lines unfunny.

The comic refused to do the show. She realized, correctly, that certain unfunny elements are required to make the funny parts funny.

In some cases, the setup can be omitted because it has been so well developed by the comedian. Jack Benny, the legendary vaudeville, radio, and television personality, spent his entire career establishing the image of himself as a cheapskate. He rarely had to furnish that information as a prerequisite to some of his punch lines. One classic example, which is reported to be the longest laugh in broadcast history, was when Benny was confronted by a robber. The crook came up behind Benny, threatened him with a gun, and said:

Your money or your life.

The audience roared because they knew that Jack Benny was such a penny-pincher that this was a serious dilemma for him.

After the gangster repeated the line, Jack replied with:

I'm thinking it over.

The comedy routine worked because no one had to remind the audience that "Jack Benny was so cheap that…"

Dean Martin, after he separated from Jerry Lewis, developed the comedy persona of a heavy drinker. Everyone was aware of that. Consequently, he didn't have to give out that information when he said:

I once shook hands with Pat Boone and my whole right side sobered up.

Essential information also can be carried over from previous parts of a comic's routine. Consider the following string of jokes:

I have a friend who is the cheapest man in the world. He holds onto money so long he has a dollar bill … the picture on it is of George Washington when he was a boy.

They say that crime doesn't pay, but if it goes to lunch with this guy, it will.

On his first date with his future wife, he took her out for coffee and donuts. She was thrilled. She had never donated blood before.

When he finally did take her out for drinks, she said, "I guess I'll have champagne." He said, "Guess again."

The required information is presented in the first gag—"I have a friend who is the cheapest man in the world." That information, that setup, obtains for the rest of the series of gags.

This Fifth Commandment, though, still must feel rather vague. How short should a joke be? How long can a joke continue without violating this precept? A rule of thumb that was mentioned earlier was to keep a joke as short as it can be and still remain a joke. Admittedly, that too can seem unclear.

It might be better to forget about short and long and think rather in terms of economics. Suppose someone asked you if you thought $750 was too much to pay. You would ask, "For what?" You would want to know what you're getting for your money. For a new, large screen TV, it might be a good price. For a new shirt, it would seem a little steep. What you're buying determines what you should reasonably pay.

There is a certain economy of comedy, too. The audience listens to your setup for a certain amount of time, then they get the punch line. They must sense that the value of the punch line justifies the amount of time they spent listening to the setup. If the preamble to the gag rambles on and on and the punch line is weak, the audience feels cheated. These are "shaggy dog" stories, or jokes that you might call "groaners." The audience wanted better *value* for the time they invested.

Of course, sometimes "concise" is in the eye of the deliverer. The style and the speech patterns of the comic may determine how long or how short a gag is. Some comics have the ability to carry a joke out for some time and still deliver worthwhile punch at the end. Other comics have a machine-gun style of comedy delivery and timing. That's up to the individual comic.

In general, though, being concise means giving the audience all of the information they need to appreciate and understand your punch line, but not giving them unnecessary information. Certainly, it's not being concise to give them useless, irrelevant information. That only detracts from the punch line.

Consider the following line:

> *I wanted my wife to take an interest in my activities. You know a lot of men claim that their wives never take an interest in their activities. They don't care about their business, or their hobbies. They don't want to hear stories about their golf games. They don't care how things are going at the office. I wanted my wife to be different, to take an interest in what I do. So she hired a detective.*

That's too much information. It detracts from the punch. Isn't it much cleaner, shorter, and more effective to say simply:

> *I wanted my wife to take an interest in my activities. So she did. She hired a detective.*

So, in conclusion, remember this simple guideline to being concise: A joke that should be short and is, is better than a joke that should be short and isn't.

VI

THOU SHALT CREATE
A VIVID IMAGE

It seems as though comics work with words. They have a script which is words printed on paper. They stand behind a microphone which serves to amplify the words. The audience supposedly pays attention so that they can hear every word the comedian offers them. So, in fact, comics *do* work with words. Those words, though, are only the medium that the comic uses.

An artist's medium is paint. However, it's not the paint that creates the masterpiece; it's the picture that emerges from those paints. When we gaze at the *Mona Lisa*, DaVinci's masterpiece in the Louvre, we don't see a dash of burnt sienna here and a splash of vivid blue there. No, we see the mysterious smile on the face. We see the woman.

Granted that *Mona Lisa* couldn't exist if there weren't splashes of color artfully applied here and dashes of paint skillfully brushed there. We of course recognize the technical skill of the artist, but we appreciate the culmination of that skill. We admire the painting, not the paint.

Comedy is similar. The audience is not laughing at the words the comedian uses so much as they are responding to the pictures those words paint. We're responding to the ideas that those words generate.

Most of us tend to think visually. We see a picture in our mind that represents our thoughts. Think of Thanksgiving dinner and you'll recall scenes of your family and friends gathered around a grand feast. Anticipate an upcoming vacation and you'll probably see yourself lounging around a pool or relaxing in a comfortable hotel room. Put some thought, any thought, into your mind now and see if you don't visualize a scene of that thought. We dream visually, too. Our dreams don't consist of a narrator telling us what is happening. No, we see the setting. We visualize the action. We "live" through the experience As the proverb says, "A picture is worth a thousand words." Graphic images are more powerful than verbal descriptions.

Comedy is mostly verbal. Yes, there is some humor that is purely visual. For instance, with pantomime there are no words used at all. Then there's the proverbial man slipping on a banana peel, the pie in the face, the whack over the head with a slapstick—all visual forms of humor. The audience sees the comedy and laughs at it.

However, most comedy deals with words. Jokes are either written out or recited by a comic. Humorists use words in the same manner that novelists use them—to create an image. The comedy, in general, is more effective if the comic can present a vivid image to the minds of the listeners or the readers. In most cases, it's the graphic picture that the audience responds to.

The admonition, "Thou Shalt Create a Vivid Image," does not reduce the importance of the words in a comic's presentation. Rather, it makes the proper use of words that much more critical. The purpose of this Sixth Commandment is to remind all of us that the humorist is in charge of controlling the image. Just as Leonardo DaVinci applied the paint to the canvas in order to produce an image of the smiling lady in the *Mona Lisa*, the comic should apply the words appropriately to create the image he or she wants to convey. Just as skilled writers put their words on paper in the proper sequence, using the appropriate vocabulary and syntax to describe accurately what they want the readers to "see," humorists, too, should arrange their words in an exact and proper order to present the image that they want the listeners to see in their minds.

Consider this line from Rodney Dangerfield, the late comic who claimed "I don't get no respect"—not even from his own parents. He said:

> *My father gave me a bat for Christmas. First time I tried to play with it, it flew away.*

When people hear that wonderfully funny line, they can almost see the critter flying off into the blue sky. They might even see the bewildered look on the youngster's face as his Christmas gift wings its way to freedom. There's a tiny play going on in the mind of each listener. It's graphic; it's vivid; it's alive.

Using the same concept, Dangerfield might have said:

> *My father gave me a bat for Christmas. Oh not a baseball bat; the live kind.*

This is merely a bland statement of fact. There's no picture associated with this gag. It's a statement of fact. It's a funny idea, but it has much more impact when we not only *know* that it's the flying kind, but we can see it actually flying. The visual component makes the gag funny.

Steven Wright has a magnificent line that reads:

I just added a skylight in my living room. The people in the apartment above me are furious.

The listener's mind sees that new skylight, but it also sees the folks in the apartment above looking at this glass enclosure that is in the middle of their living room floor. Whoever hears this joke can see the "furious" look on those folks as they gaze down into Steven Wright's apartment.

That's a much stronger joke than if Wright simply told us:

I was planning on putting a skylight in my living room, but I couldn't get the OK from the people in the apartment above mine.

The joke idea is still intact, but the picture that it produces is not as striking. It becomes a much weaker gag.

Kathleen Madigan had a fine line when the book *The Final Exit* was causing a stir. *The Final Exit* was a book that was supposed to be an aid to people who were considering suicide. Madigan did a routine about standing in line at the bookstore checkout counter behind a man who was purchasing the book. During this routine, she said:

This guy's going to pay $19.95 for a book on committing suicide. I said, "Hey, I'll stab you in the head for five bucks."

It's a wonderfully funny gag. Consider, though, if Madigan had said:

This guy's going to pay $19.95 for a book on committing suicide. I said, "Hey, I'll kill you for five bucks."

The comedy concept is the same, but the image created isn't vivid. How will she "kill him?" Strangling, shooting, beating, poisoning? The image is vague, not as intense.

A less powerful image leads to a less powerful joke

The original wording presents a definite, more accurate, more graphic picture, and it creates a much stronger gag.

Words are the medium that the humorist uses, but in most cases, it's the mental picture those words create that reinforces the laugh. A good comedy concept accompanied by a vivid picture produces the most satisfying response. That's why the Sixth Commandment proclaims "Thou Shalt Create a Vivid Image."

VII

Thou Shalt Let the Audience Know When to Laugh

It seems almost axiomatic that when a comic takes the stage all he or she wants is to hear laughter from the audience. However, that's not true. Well, perhaps it's true, but only partially. As Alex Trebek likes to say on *Jeopardy*, "Be more specific."

There are different types of laughter, not all of them desirable from a performer's point of view. There's the laughter of ridicule. This is when the audience, or someone in the audience, is scoffing at the performer for *trying* to be funny, rather than appreciating their being funny. It's a scornful cackle that seems to be saying, "You're so incompetent at what you're attempting that I can't help but snicker." This is not welcomed by the comic.

There's a sympathy laugh. This is from a table of relatives or friends who respond to the performance more out of loyalty than genuine enjoyment. It sounds forced, hollow, insincere, and usually serves to highlight the inadequacy of the performance rather than enhancing it. This type of laughter is also not desirable to the comedian.

There's shallow, sporadic response from the listeners. A few people on one side of the room may chuckle at one gag; a table on the other side of the room may giggle at another joke or two. There's no consistency to the audience response. It emphasizes the inconsistency of the act and of the material. No comic is happy with this type of reaction.

Perhaps most disconcerting is that laughter that seems to be out of sync. It comes at the wrong times. A comic may be reciting a setup line and several people in the audience begin reacting. Who knows why. Yet it's there. The laughter may be genuine, but it's distracting to the rest of the audience, who are still waiting for the real punch line, and to the performer, who's waiting to deliver it.

These are all undeniably forms of laughter, but you can see why a good comic would rather do without them.

What a comic wants is predictable, coordinated laughter, for the people to react genuinely, at the proper time, and all together. The comedian wants the crowd to respond when he or she wants them to respond, not before and not later. If the crowd is to laugh on cue, someone must give them their cue. Someone must provide the impetus to laughter. Someone must *tell them when to laugh*. That someone is the comic.

To illustrate this, picture a comedy magician walking onstage after being introduced. Without a word to the audience, he begins his first illusion. He goes through all the dramatic gestures to impress the viewers. However, as he performs there is an unexpected reaction from the audience. Folks begin to snicker. It's a self-conscious, embarrassed type of suppressed chuckling running through the theater. It's almost as if people don't want to laugh, but they can't stop themselves.

The magician senses the reaction. He knows that something is amiss, but is not sure exactly what it is. Then he glances down and sees the reason. His fly is open and the shirttail of his white shirt is hanging out of it. It's too obvious for the audience to miss.

The comic magician seems embarrassed by the obvious *faux pas*. He turns his back to the audience and we see him going through some movements that indicate that he is tucking his shirttail in and zipping his fly. When he turns back to face the crowd, the shirttail is still hanging out from his open fly. This time, though, it is bright red instead of white.

The audience erupts in solid, genuine, appreciative laughter. They're all roaring openly, unashamedly, and as a unit. And they are responding for a reason. That reason is that the comic performer wanted them to react with laughter. He told them when to laugh.

It's almost as if he is saying to them, "The white shirttail was the setup to my joke. That was the misdirection. I wanted you to believe that I had left my fly open inadvertently. All of you fell for it; you bought it hook, line, and sinker. This, the red shirttail, is the punch line. Magicians often change silks from one color to another. I tricked you by changing my shirttail from white to red. This is the surprise I present to you. This is where I want you to laugh." And they do.

Even though the first part of this particular comic piece was done on purpose—it was the comedian setting up the real gag to come—it highlights the difference in the audience response. In the setup, when the audience thought the comic had simply forgotten to zip his fly, the reaction was sporadic and subdued. Some people started to laugh when they noticed it. However, different people reacted at different times. Should they laugh when they first saw it? Should they laugh as the magician continued his act, oblivious to his shirttail hanging out? Should they refrain from laughing in order not to further embarrass the performer? Should someone shout out from the audience, "Your fly is open?" You can appreciate that there is indecision. No one in the crowd really knows what to do or when to do it.

But when that comic turns around and the crowd sees that he has "magically" transformed the white shirttail to a red shirttail, everyone knows exactly what to do. They laugh. They've been told to laugh and they obey.

You may have heard it said of a talented comedian, "He could get laughs just reading the telephone book." It's a tremendous compliment to the performer's talent. Unfortunately, it's not true. Well, it might be true, but it has to be qualified. We'll discuss that in just a little while.

Some performers, though, have actually tried this gimmick. One came on stage, sat on a stool, opened a local telephone book, and spent his entire set simply reading from it in a monotone. Admittedly, it's funny to hear about such a prank. But when you're in the audience for such a bizarre presentation, how should you react? When do you laugh? Even if you appreciate the humor of someone attempting this, when do you laugh? Do you realize how bizarre this is after the fifth name is read? After twenty names, maybe you begin to chuckle. After a half-hour of this recitation, you'll grow tired of chuckling. Most likely no one in the audience will roar with raucous laughter. It's an amusing gimmick to hear about; not so entertaining to sit through.

Earlier we did say that some comics might be talented enough to get genuine laughs from reading from an actual phone book. However, they would probably do it by *triggering* laughter. For instance, if a comic were doing this, he or she might start boring themselves. That entertainer might start to get drowsy and actually feign falling asleep and then snap awake. This could prompt the audience to laugh. The comic might do that once or twice, and then the third time actually fall off the stool onto the floor. That would probably get belly laughs.

This comedian is now *telling* the audience when to laugh. No longer is the performer simply reading the phone book; the performer is doing comedy chunks based on the idea of reading from the phone book. Each of these bits is triggering a response from the audience.

Humorists, whether writers or performers, have one primary goal: to generate laughter. It's their responsibility. They must organize their routines to draw guffaws from an audience. But that response should be controlled and coordinated. The humorist must orchestrate the listener reactions just as a choral director must orchestrate the voices. Obviously, they should all sing the same song, in the same key, and to the same tempo.

So humorists want the response to be orchestrated. They want the entire audience (or at least a goodly portion of it) to explode, as a unit, with genuine, appreciative laughter. If you want organization, someone has to organize it. Who better than the person at the microphone? The person standing in the spotlight. The person who should be controlling the room.

It's apparent that if you want a group of people to laugh together, you must tell them *when* to laugh. That's the message of this Seventh Commandment.

Jokes should have a built-in laugh trigger: the punch line. The sole purpose of any joke is to deliver a solid punch line. All the words in the joke—whether it's a quick one-liner or a longer anecdote—are there to support the punch line. So the words that lead to that punch, and the location of that punch, determine how well you can signal an audience that it's time to laugh.

In order to send a strong signal, the humorist should be sure that the words he or she chooses are effective and accurate. The words in the setup of the gag are just as important as the key word in the punch line.

The position of the key word—the one that delivers the surprise or the twist—is important in telling the audience when to laugh. Usually you want the punch line as close to the end of the joke as possible. Otherwise it can be confusing. The punch line is telling the listeners it's time to laugh, but if you continue talking, they're not sure whether to laugh or listen. You're stepping on your own laughs.

One comedian delivered a line about how he was thrilled to have become a success because he could now help his family. He said:

> *Mom, you've been bending over a hot stove all your life. Straighten up.*

It's a nice gag that certainly triggers audience laughter. Consider the following variation, though:

> *Mom, I really would like to see you straighten up. You know, you've been bending over a hot stove all your life.*

There's no real place there for the audience to realize they should laugh. It's a much weaker gag.

Another comic once said:

> *I've been rich and I've been poor. Rich is better.*

It's a funny line and people know where to laugh. It's a much better form than the following:

> *I'll tell you I much prefer being rich to being
> poor. I've been both.*

The joke is weakened by relocating the punch line and probably won't elicit a single laugh.

The punch line is the reason for a joke to exist. The words leading up to that punch, the location of the punch, and the words that are part of it, are all important. They are the key to telling the listeners when to laugh. They generate explosive laughter that is organized, yet seems spontaneous. You the humorist have to organize the audience response. You do that by following this Seventh Commandment, "Thou Shalt Tell the Audience When to Laugh."

VIII

Thou Shalt Use Solid References

Below are some typical gags. Read them over and see if you can discover a similarity among them:

> *I used to date our town librarian. Every time I asked her to marry me, she said, "Sssshhhh!"*

> *They call it a family tree because if you look hard enough, you'll always be able to find some sap in it.*

> *My husband is no handyman. I asked him to hang a picture for me once. He tied a piece of rope around it and kicked a chair out from under it.*

> *I made a peanut butter sandwich in the microwave once. It sticks to the roof of your mouth much faster.*

> *My husband does absolutely nothing around the house. I get the feeling I married a knick-knack.*

Have you uncovered the common thread? It's that all of them are composed of two parts—the basic idea and an idea that is related to that. In the first one, the librarian is related to someone who is always demanding silence. The second ties in a family tree with a real tree that has sap in it. The third gag compares hanging a picture with an actual hanging. The fourth compares making a normal peanut butter sandwich with the quickness of making a microwave peanut butter sandwich. The fifth joke compares an inactive husband to an inactive household ornament. All of them take one idea and compare it to another idea. The majority of gags do just that.

Of course, simply referring one concept to another doesn't make a joke. For instance:

Her eyes sparkled like diamonds

He was as strong as an ox

These are comparisons, but they're not funny. Jokes are separate ideas that are tied together in a unique and creative way. It's the humorist who must supply the creativity that makes the comparisons entertaining. Consider:

Her eyes sparkled like diamonds. They matched her necklace, her earrings, and the price she charged for getting to know her better.

He was as strong as an ox ... and just about as attractive.

The comparisons are still there, but they now have an added twist—a surprise that makes them funny.

Note, too, that not all relationships are similar in nature. Consider the following:

He had the intelligence of a ping-pong ball.

A ping pong ball is far from an intelligent creature, yet the comparison works. To turn it into a joke, one might say:

> *He had the intelligence of a ping-pong ball, but not nearly the personality.*

Here's another gag that connects one idea to a totally dissimilar idea, yet it seems the difference between the ideas ties them together:

> *Alcohol has never solved any problems. But then again, neither has milk.*

Simply relating two ideas together, as we discussed, doesn't create a funny line. It takes creativity and talent for a humorist to provide the cleverness that generates the comedy. Nevertheless, the references—the ideas that can relate to the main premise—are the starting point for the creativity. In order to relate one idea to another in a unique, clever, and funny manner, you must begin with the ideas that relate to one another. These are the *references*.

References, as relating to gags, are those things that are associated with the primary idea. Again, they may be associated by being similar or by being dissimilar. To illustrate this, take the main idea that a person is a cheapskate. Some things that might be related to that concept are that he still has his first dollar, that he never opens his wallet, that he refuses to buy anything, that he'll do anything to avoid spending money, that he never pays his debts, and so on—an almost infinite number of other references. However, even these few can help the humorist to generate laughs. For example:

This guy is so cheap, he buys one Christmas card each year and sends it out in the form of a chain letter.

Cheap? His hearing aid is on a party line. — Henny Youngman

This guy still has the first dollar he ever borrowed.

My friend always leaves a twenty percent tip. Twenty percent of what anybody else would leave.

This guy is so cheap he won't even buy deodorant. He buys that soap that odor proofs the body for 12 hours and then keeps turning his clock back.

To be effective, the references should be descriptive. They should convey the thought that the comic wants the audience to hear. For instance, here are a few witty country sayings that describe *uselessness*:

He was about as useful as a trap door in a canoe.

He was about as useful as a back pocket on a shirt.

He was about as useful as a pogo stick in quicksand.

Notice that each of the above items would serve no purpose whatsoever. That's exactly what the humorists wants those references to say. The primary idea in these quotes is *uselessness*. The references describe that idea quite well.

Here's a one-liner that accomplishes the mission effectively, also. The primary idea here is that airlines may not be as safe as people claim they are.

> If flying is supposed to be the safest form of travel, how come you don't see insurance vending machines outside of bicycle shops?

The references should translate well, too. In other words, the ideas should apply equally to the primary idea, and the idea used in the reference. For instance:

> Men are like steel. When they lose their temper, they lose their worth.

The concept expressed works just as well for "men" as it does for "steel." Yes, it does utilize a play on the word "temper," but it still applies to both sides of the equation. However, a gag like the following doesn't quite translate:

> Our airline flight was like riding a school bus. It stopped at every corner.

That does get across the idea that the flight may have been slow and tedious, but it is hard to visualize an airplane stopping at street corners.

References are the quarry from which the raw material for the gags is mined. It's beneficial for the humorist to uncover an abundance of usable references. That doesn't imply that quantity is preferable to quality in humor. It does, though, suggest that quantity can influence quality. The more references the humorist can uncover, presumably, the more gags that humorist can create. It seems obvious that the larger the pool, the better the top few gags will be that are selected from it.

This Eighth Commandment of Comedy dictates that a good quantity of solid references will improve both the quality and quantity of the jokes. Effective references should convey the idea that the humorist wants to convey. They should apply equally to the primary idea and to the punch line. They should be understood by the listeners. And, of course, they should be funny. That, however, depends on the skill, the talent, and the genius of the humorist. The references are not the jokes. They are joke ideas that the humorist must convert to clever lines.

IX

THOU SHALT REMEMBER
THE AUDIENCE

Two important components of comedy are the skill of the performer and the quality of the material. You need top-notch funny material and a comic who can deliver the lines with talent and gusto. A worthwhile entertainer can be ineffective with a substandard script. Conversely, great material can be destroyed with weak execution. It takes a blend of solid writing and a compelling presentation to make comedy work. Nevertheless there is a third element that cannot be ignored: the audience.

Jokes are the basic building block of humor. Jokes are to humor as bricks are to a building. The jokes are not the structure, but they are the units that compose the structure. They are the bricks that build monologues, sketches, sitcoms, humorous plays, teleplays, and screenplays.

But what is a joke? Basically, a joke is anything that makes people laugh. It might be a witty saying or it could be total silence at just the right time. It could be a funny movement or complete inactivity. A joke could be a change in tone of voice. It could be a look. It might be a scream. Whatever its form, it's a joke if it makes people laugh.

The key word in that description is "people." Every humorist needs an audience. Humor requires laughter and if there are no people there can be no laughter. Philosophers ask: "If a tree falls in the forest and there is no one there to hear it, does it make a noise?" Who knows? But if there is no one there to laugh at it, it definitely does not make a joke.

An audience is essential. Obviously, you can't have laughter without someone laughing. Some may object that a humorous writer doesn't have an audience near the keyboard howling at each clever phrase that's typed. Some may say that performers in a comedy film don't have people sitting out front reacting to each funny move or line. But each has a potential or eventual audience. The writer at the keyboard is writing to his or her readers. The witticisms are aimed at them. The jokes are there for the readers' future enjoyment. Similarly, actors filming a movie perform for those folks who will buy tickets and fill the theater seats. Humor cannot exist without an audience.

Whether developing a joke in private or delivering it on a stage, the humorist must remember and include the audience. But how?

First, the comic must make sure the listeners *understand* the comedy. He must speak to them in language that they comprehend and about topics that they are aware of. If the audience doesn't understand what the comedian is saying, they can't be expected to laugh (refer back to the Third Commandment).

Second, it's essential that the audience *appreciate* the humor. They must recognize the irony, the connections, the inconsistencies—whatever makes the gag funny. They must have a frame of reference that coincides with the comic's material. A specific audience must "get" the specific gag in order to laugh at it.

Third, the listeners should agree with the comedy. A funny joke is not a funny joke unless the audience agrees that it's a funny joke. Humorists may take exception to this, but the audience is the final arbitrator. As an example, consider this gag:

> *A speaker asked a gentlemen, "Why are you a Democrat?" The man replied, "My Daddy was a Democrat and his Daddy before him was a Democrat and that's why I'm a Democrat." The speaker said, "Let me ask you—if you're Daddy was a jackass and his Daddy before him was a jackass, what would that make you?" The man said, "A Republican."*

That's a funny and fairly innocuous joke, but probably not one you should tell at a Republican National Convention. Why not? Because the attendees will probably neither agree with nor approve of your implication.

Part of using your audience effectively is to give them what they *want to hear*. This doesn't mean that a humorist must pander to an audience. It doesn't imply that the comic should change his or her standards in order to cater to the audience's philosophy. It does suggest that the humorist avoid offending his or her audience by excluding material that they would prefer not to hear.

Remember a comic's job is to generate laughter. If the material doesn't produce laughs, but the comic insists on presenting it anyway, then that comic is not being a comic. He or she may be a philosopher or a campaigner or a demagogue or an agitator, but not a humorist.

Referring to the example above, if you tell that gag at a Republican National Convention it will probably get boos and hisses. However, reverse the titles, ending the gag with the punch line "The man said, 'A Democrat,'" and the line will get huge laughs and probably appreciative applause. Now the audience agrees with and approves of your implication.

"Remembering your audience" often demands that you know something about your audience. The more information a comic can gather about the listeners, the more he or she can write material that will be appropriate for that particular crowd. There are different degrees of this.

The ultimate would be a "Roast," where the humorist is paying tribute to a specific person that everyone in the audience knows and knows about. The Friars Roasts or the old televised Dean Martin roasts are examples of this type of presentation. Here the gags are aimed at a specific target. All of the listeners understand the comedy and it is exactly what they want to hear—someone poking fun at the guest of honor.

Another degree of knowing the audience would be if a comic is working to a specific audience, for instance one like the Washington Press Club dinner. The humorist in this case knows that the people out front are all connected with journalism and politics. His or her material can be geared specifically to those topics. Another example would be if the comic is working to a specific group of people: a chiropractors' convention, a mystery writers' banquet, a national pharmacists' seminar, or the like.

For example, consider this gag delivered at an insurance salesmen's national convention:

> *It's easy to tell this is an insurance salesmen's convention. I asked someone in the lobby how to get to the banquet hall and he said, "Go down this*

*corridor and turn right, but God forbid if anything
should happen to you, how's the little woman
going to get there?"*

That line played well because this audience understood the lingo, appreciated the content, agreed with the
humor, and understood that the gag was aimed specifically at them.

A comic can also gear material to a particular audience when working in a specific locale. For example, a
comic working on a cruise ship obviously has listeners
who are also on a cruise ship. Certain material can cater
to this definite audience. Humorists who work on college
campuses can be aware of some of the details of that
particular campus and they can utilize that knowledge.
When Bob Hope visited various bases on his military
tours, he always had his writers research facts about each
specific location. The writers uncovered the unsavory
neighborhoods nearby and used those in gags. They
kidded the commanding officer. They learned much of
the scuttlebutt about the camp and included that in the
routines. The audience appreciated the humor that much
more because it incorporated them and their base into
the show.

A more general locale can also offer the comic the
opportunity to remember the audience. If a comic is
working in Detroit, for example, he or she can uncover
what the people of that city are concerned with at this
time. Jokes about whatever interests them will get a little
added boost in audience response.

Finally, there are those times when the audience
is completely undefined. For instance, if a comic is
appearing on a nationally televised show, there is no way
to know who is watching. In that case, the comic is forced
to go with more general material.

A final aspect of the Ninth Commandment is to always pay attention to your audience. The audience is the judge of your comedy material, so if you have alternative versions of a gag, try them out. Let the audience reaction decide which is the most effective. And remember: The audience evaluates not only the material, but your *presentation* of the material. Which is the best way to tell a joke? Where should you pause? How long should you pause? If you listen to the audience, they can offer immediate feedback on your performance, giving you a chance to make adjustments.

The road to comedy success is to present an entertaining act, and then keep making it better. Your audience can help you improve, if you listen to them.

It's beneficial in any performance for the comic to be aware that the audience is as much a part of the comedy as the material and the delivery. That is why the Ninth Commandment dictates that "Thou Shalt Remember the Audience."

X

THOU SHALT BE CLEVER

An important component of comedy is the genius of the humorist. Humor exists all around, in every person, every place, and every situation. However, it takes a wit to uncover it and express it persuasively. The Tenth Commandment of Comedy is a plea for all humorists to couch their comments as cleverly as they can. Be unique, be inventive, be entertaining, be funny.

One comic did just that with the line:

> *Anytime you see a man open the car door for his wife, you know either the car is new or the wife is.*

George Carlin perceptively observed:

> *Think of how stupid the average person is, and realize that half of them are stupider than that.*

He also noted:

> *Have you ever noticed that the lawyer always smiles more than the client?*

People recognize the basic truth of these statements, agree with them, enjoy them, and laugh at them—but not until a comic has pointed them out. It is the humorist's job to observe, research, and uncover the everyday ironies that exist all around us. Humor is there, waiting to be mined and refined.

Then it must be delivered to an audience. As with the development of a joke, the delivery, too, depends on the deft touch of the comic. The humor cannot just be shared with the listeners or readers; it must be revealed in a clever, unique, entertaining manner.

One musician was dissatisfied with his gig. He told the bandleader he wanted to quit. The bandleader pointed out that contractually he couldn't just quit; he had to give two-weeks' notice. So the musician said:

> *Four weeks from now, when you look for me on the bandstand, I will have been gone two.*

Often it's the phrasing that transforms a statement into a joke. The more cleverly you can phrase a gag, the more effective it will be. This Tenth Commandment implores the humorist to find the most inventive, enlightening, and entertaining way to present the comic concept. Charles Schultz, the creator of the comic strip *Peanuts*, said a similar thing about cartoonists. In this slightly paraphrased quote, he asked: "Why do they put down the first idea they come to? Why don't they think a little deeper and come up with something really creative and original?"

Following are a couple of examples.

It's hard to pinpoint "cleverness" or where it comes from, but we do recognize it when we see it. And we appreciate it.

At one comedy writing class, the students were asked to come up with a line that showed how troubled Vincent Van Gogh was all his life. In fact, that may have led to his cutting off his ear. One student came up with the following:

Vincent Van Gogh was problematic even as a child. Everything his Mother said to him went in one ear and out the same one.

Another writer in the class came up with this:

He was probably depressed because in his entire life he sold only one painting. Even then, he only made enough money to buy one ear muff.

By thinking a little deeper, these writers were able to generate lines that were truly creative, original, and funny. They not only followed Charles Schulz's admonition, but also the Tenth Commandment—Thou Shalt Be Clever.

COMEDY CHECKLIST FOR INDIVIDUAL GAGS

1. Does your gag include a "twist," a misdirection, something unexpected, a strong effective surprise for your listeners, preferably towards the end of the joke?

2. Will the listeners readily recognize and accept the truth of your comment or the truth that it is based on?

3. Can your audience understand the language, the references, the context, and the meaning of your joke?

4. Have you avoided outdated references in your gag? Can you update to more current references?

5. Is your joke concise? Does it supply enough information for the audience to appreciate the humor, but not so much information that it detracts from the impact of the comedy?

6. Does the verbal presentation of your gag allow the audience to form a graphic image in their minds?

7. Have you, the humorist, controlled the audience response? Have you told the audience when to laugh?

8. Have you used strong, appropriate references in your joke? Are they references that effectively convey your meaning to the listeners?

9. Is your comedy consistent with the audience's frame of reference and point of view? Does it capitalize on them?

10. Have you tried to phrase your comedy concept in a unique, clever, entertaining way? Have you tried to word the gag in such a way as to maximize the audience response?

About the Author

Since the early 1960s, **Gene Perret** has been writing comedy material for such legendary performers as Bob Hope, Phyllis Diller, Carol Burnett, Tim Conway, and others. He has been awarded three Emmys and one Writer's Guild Award for his work on *The Carol Burnett Show* writing staff.

Perret has also helped start the careers of many television comedy writers through his books, conferences, and classes. For information about Gene Perret's other books and teaching, visit his website:

ComedyWritersRoom.com.

More Great Books for Writers by GENE PERRET

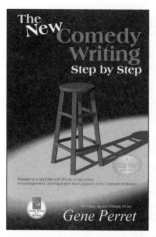